BEAR THE CHALLENGE

Stories About Children Who Did!

Stories by
Megan J. Stoll
M.A. Kokos Lambrou

Poems by
Norah Scannell

Llumina Press

ISBN: 1-932560-31-9
Printed in the United States of America by Llumina Press

ABOUT THE FOUNDATION

Bear Necessities Pediatric Cancer Foundation, Inc. is a not-for-profit organization founded in 1992 to help provide hope for todays and tomorrows. Inspired by the valiant struggle of an eight-year-old cancer patient, Barrett "Bear" Krupa, who battled the disease for six years, Bear Necessities was established by "Bear's" mother, Kathleen Casey, his sister Courtney, and by "Bear" himself before he lost his battle in 1993.

Bear Necessities' mission is to encourage, supplement and initiate research on a national level, directly related to pediatric cancer, to enhance hospital support services offered to children and their families and to provide special assistance to pediatric cancer patients through our Small Miracle Program.

The Small Miracle Program was developed to support pediatric cancer patients and their families living in and/or being treated in Illinois, as they face the many physical, psychological and financial challenges that accompany the diagnosis and treatment of cancer. The goal is to brighten one moment of one day by fulfilling dreams and creating Small Miracles for them!

On behalf of "Bear" and children everywhere stricken with cancer, thank you for your kindness and for adding another today and tomorrow to so many lives.

TABLE OF CONTENTS

We dedicate this book to its inspiration,
Larry Dunn, who is truly an example
of how to Bear the Challenge *of Pediatric Cancer,*
and to the children and families
who must face and overcome
the many obstacles that this disease creates.

Papou's Magic Ring

By M.A. Kokos Lambrou

"Happy birthday to you, happy birthday to you, happy birthday dear Tommy, happy birthday to you!"

As I leaned forward to blow out my candles, I wished for my tenth birthday to be extra special. I was already excited because my parents were taking my sister and me to Greece this summer. We were going to an island called Lefkatha. That is where my Papou lives. When I blew out my candles in one huge breath, my body tingled, and I got this strange feeling all over. It only lasted a second, and then it was gone.

"Okay, Tommy, let me cut the cake for everyone," Mom said as she gently moved me out of the way.

Forget the cake, I thought, *I want to open my presents!* I ran to the couch where all the presents were patiently waiting, and I started to bring them back to the table. "Tommy, let's make sure everyone has their cake, *before* you start opening your gifts," Mom sounded a bit annoyed that I was so anxious.

"You only turn ten once, Mom. Let me start, pleeeease?" I begged.

Mom tilted her head to one side, and gave me that motherly smile, and said, "Okay, if you want to open presents now, that's fine. Just let me grab the camera."

I had so many presents in front of me; I didn't know which one to start with. Should I start with the largest box, and work my way to the smaller ones? Or should I start with the smallest box, and work my way to the larger ones? People always say that good things come in small packages, so I decided to start with the largest box first. The largest box was a rectangular shape. It was very long and short. I had absolutely no idea what it could be. I didn't hesitate to keep myself or anyone else in suspense; I just ripped off the wrapping paper as fast as I could. A big, brown rectangular shaped box. I still didn't know what was inside, so I did what any ten year old boy would do, I yanked open the box as quickly as I could. My heart was racing, and I couldn't wait to see what was inside. "Wow! I can't believe it! An air hockey table! You are the best, Uncle John! I really love it! Thank you, thank you!" I exclaimed. I was hoping that some adult would put it together so that I could play on it soon. The next box, a race track set. The next, Legos. The next and next, clothes and more clothes. I started getting down to smaller and smaller boxes. Some of the smaller boxes had CD's, video games, books, and sports stuff. As I looked around, I realized that I had opened all of the gifts. Now, I was hoping that Uncle John would put together the air hockey table for me. "Uncle Johnnie, are you up for a game of air hockey?" I asked.

"You got it kid. I'll go downstairs and set up the table right now," he replied.

"Ah, hold on a second," Dad said. "I have one last very special gift that came a very long way to get here."

Gee, more presents? I wonder what this is all about.

"Tommy," my dad explained as he held out a very small box, "This gift came all the way from Lefkatha, and it's from Papou."

"Why is Papou sending me a gift here? Aren't we going to see him in a couple of weeks?" I asked.

"Yes, we will see him soon, but he wanted you to open this on your tenth birthday," Dad said.

Another present? I wasn't going to ask why. Who wouldn't want another present? After all, good things come in small packages. This package was very small; so that means it must be "extra good!"

I held out my hand to receive the gift from my dad. When the small package was placed in my palm, it happened again. I felt that strange tingling sensation all over my body. This time, it seemed to last longer than when I was blowing out my candles. My stomach dropped, just the way it does when you are on a roller coaster, going down, down, down. I waited a moment before I opened it. "Go on, open it Tommy. Let's see what Papou has sent you," Mom was getting anxious.

I carefully unwrapped the paper at the seams. Fear told me to do so. Who knows, if I touched this little box the wrong way, I could get that strange feeling again. Everyone started to crowd around me. They were leaning in so close, that I could feel them breathing on my arm. A white box came through once I tediously took off the wrapping paper. Gently, I lifted the cover to the white box. Inside I found yet another box. This one was black. It had kind of a fuzzy feeling to it when I reached in to take it out. This was it. This little black, almost fuzzy box came all the way from Greece. The box fit nicely in the palm of my hand. I placed the other hand on top to open it up. At a snail's pace, I opened the box. Something shone brightly in my eyes, and I had to look away for a second. Everyone around me let out a gasp.

"Oh, my goodness," I was in awe. Before I could say anything else, my dad spoke. "Tommy, the ring in that box is a very special ring. Your Papou is giving it to you because you will carry on the family name. This ring has been in our family for years. It is what is considered an heirloom. You see, your Papou received it from his Papou, who received it from his Papou. It may be a little big on you now, but you will have it for many years."

"Wow, that is special. I can't wait to see Papou, and tell him how much I love it!" In a flash, I took the ring out of the box, and put it on my finger. It happened again. This time the tingling sensation was so strong, that I had to sit down to overcome it. The room looked like it was spinning. When my mother stuck her face in front of mine, to ask me how I liked it, I saw three of her. I closed my eyes, and shook my head. "Are you okay dear?" Mother asked.

After I opened my eyes, everything seemed normal again, "Yeah Ma, I'm fine." As I looked down at my finger, I said, "Dad, you were right, this ring is too big for me. I love it so much that I want to wear it now. That way I can feel that Papou is always with me. How can we make it fit better?"

"Here Tommy, give me the ring, and I'll put cloth around the back to make it fit, for now," Mom said. I gave my mother the ring, and went in the basement to play air hockey with Uncle John.

After the party was over, I thanked everyone for coming, and told them how much I liked the gifts they gave me. I took another look at Papou's ring before I went to bed that night. I didn't want to put it on again, because I wasn't sure what kind of strange feeling I would get. Mom came to tuck me into bed, "You must be tired. You had quite a party tonight."

"Yes, I am a little tired. Thanks for the party Mom. I really had a lot of fun. Good night," I said as I gave my mom a hug and kiss. After Mom turned out the lights, I snuggled under my covers, but I didn't fall asleep right away. I kept thinking about those strange tingling sensations I had at my party. I was wondering if they really happened, or if it was my imagination because I was so excited. I decided that it was probably just my imagination, and that I should get to sleep. The next morning, I had school.

"Aw, c'mon Mom, please!" I begged.

"Don't you understand, Tommy? That ring has been in our family for years. It is an heirloom. You cannot wear it to school. The last thing we need you to do is lose the ring, or ruin it. Your papou would be very, very upset if anything happened to that ring. The answer is absolutely not," Mom stated.

I decided not to argue with my mom. She seemed a little crabby.

"Okay Mom, I won't wear it to school," I said sadly.

After I was ready for school, I took another look at the ring. I really, really wanted to take it to school and show all my friends. I hesitated, and then I put the ring into the pocket of my jeans. I felt kind of bad for a second, because my mom told me not to, but I thought if I were very careful, she'd never know. After all, I just turned ten-years-old. I could start making some of my own decisions. I felt so proud of Papou's ring, I could hardly wait to show all the kids at school!

"Tommy, time to go," Mom called out. In a flash, I was out the door and in the car. Mom pulled up to school. "Have a good day Tommy," she said.

"I certainly will," I replied with a smile. I kissed Mom good-bye, and I dashed into the school building. The first safe chance I got, I took the ring from my pocket and put it on my finger. *Uh, oh. It's happening again. Everything around me is spinning. Everything sounds like an echo.* I inched my way to the wall and held on. *Maybe if I just stand in one place, the spinning will stop.* I felt as if I were being punished because I disobeyed my mom and took the ring to school. All of a sudden, my friend Bruce whacked me on the back of my head. "What's happening, Tommy?" he asked. The whack on the head made the room stop spinning.

"Uh, oh, hi Bruce. What's up?"

Before I could say anything more, Bruce exclaimed, "What in the world do you have on your finger?" I couldn't believe that he noticed the ring so quickly. I proudly told him about my heirloom. However, Bruce didn't seem to be impressed. He said, "I thought rings were for girls. And besides, that thing is so big, it looks like you could fit all of your fingers through it!"

"Oh Bruce, you are just jealous that you don't have an heirloom!" I replied back.

"Whatever," Bruce replied.

I proceeded to the classroom and went to my desk. Bruce must have told the other kids right away, because I could see them looking at me and laughing. It bothered me that the other kids didn't know how special the ring was. I had to think of something to tell them, to make them stop making fun of me. I had a thought, and asked my teacher if I could share the ring with the class. As soon as everyone was settled, I went to the front of the room to share. "I can see that most of you noticed the ring I have on my finger this morning. I wanted to take a moment and explain to you how special this ring is to me." My heart was beating rapidly as I looked around the room and saw many faces smirking at me. I continued, "Yesterday was my tenth birthday. We had a big party at my house to celebrate. I received many, many gifts, but this one came all the way from Lefkatha, Greece. My papou sent it from Lefkatha. This ring is special because it has been in our family for years and years. My papou received it from his papou who received it from his papou. Since I'm the boy in the family who will carry on the family name, my papou gave it to me. He felt that turning ten was a special time to give it to me. You see, what I'm wearing is an heirloom. And I'm very honored to have it." Before I could say anything more, one of the boys in class shouted out, "What is a Papou?" My teacher was annoyed by the fact that one of her students shouted out, but quickly explained that Papou is the Greek word for Grandfather.

Then I continued, "Thank you Mrs. Storyheart, Papou *is* the Greek word for Grandfather. Now that we have that clear, I'd like to tell you a little more about my precious heirloom. With this ring I have special magical powers!" The whole class laughed at once. Mrs. Storyheart let out a little laugh of her own. I put on my most serious face and said, "Yes, I know it is hard to believe, but the ring is magical. I cannot reveal its powers, or else they won't work." I was hoping that my classmates would now realize how very special this ring was. One of the girls said, "Tommy, I think the only power that ring has is that it makes you a little silly!" The others in the class giggled. My plan of sharing was not going in the direction that I wanted it to. I was hoping to show the class how special the ring was, not getting made fun of even more.

Mrs. Storyheart told me that was all the time I could have, so I quickly took my seat. I really wanted to dig a hole beneath my desk and hide for the rest of the day.

There were only 6 more days of school before summer vacation. I didn't wear Papou's ring to school after that day.

****

"Do we have everything? Tickets, passports?" Mom called out to my dad.

"Yes honey, I believe we are ready to go," Dad replied.

Every part of my body was dancing. I was looking forward to going to Greece for a long time. And I was able to wear Papou's ring!

The flight to Greece was the longest I had ever experienced in my life. I wasn't sure if it was because I had to sit next to my sister for so many hours, or because I was so excited. When you are excited to go somewhere, it always seems to take longer. At any rate, I survived.

When I saw Papou, I ran like lightening. He caught me in his arms and picked me up. *Wow! Papou is still strong enough to lift me up like this! He is amazing!* After he put me down, I stuck out my hand and showed him the ring. "Papou, I just love it! I'm so proud to wear it!"

Papou had tears in his eyes, "Tommy, I want you to wear that ring and carry our good name, you hear? Having a good name is something that no one can take away from you. Someone could take out your eyeballs from their sockets, but no one, no one could ever take away your good name. I trust you now to live up to that. Do you understand?"

"Of course, Papou. You can count on me!" I said, even though I thought his whole idea about the eyeballs was a little strange.

"I bet everyone is hungry. Let's eat!" Papou exclaimed.

Like lost puppies, we all followed Papou into his dining room. He had a beautiful house. From the dining room we could see out over his balcony, which overlooked the sea. Papou never came to live with us in America, because he just loved the sea so much. We sat, we ate, and we talked for hours. I just loved listening to all the stories that Papou had to share. It was especially fun to hear about my dad when he was growing up.

After dinner, we all went out to sit on the balcony. The stars shone so beautifully in the sky. I had never seen so many stars before. I asked, "Papou, why does your sky have more stars than our sky does?"

Papou answered with a smile, "I didn't know the sky belonged to me."

"Very funny Papou, you know what I mean. How come we can see more stars here? More than we can see back home?"

"This island is not full of industry and pollution, like the big cities in America. Isn't it beautiful? I sit out here for hours at a time, just gazing."

The starlit sky didn't seem to interest the rest of my family as much as it did me. They were also very tired from the time zone changes, so they went back inside and went to sleep. Papou went in with them so that he could get them settled. I continued to star gaze. I guess I take after my Papou. After all, I was named after him.

I held onto the ring and began to twist it back and forth as I looked at the sky. The diamond in the middle of the ring seemed to be shining extra brightly. I started to get that tingling sensation all over my body again. This time it lasted longer than any other time I felt it. The brilliance of the diamond was amazing. Some kind of force locked the ring into place on my finger and angled the brilliance of the diamond straight out into the night sky and directly towards a shining star. My body froze. The last thing I remember is being lifted off my chair. How? I had no idea. I was suddenly, rapidly sucked up through the sky and closer and closer to the stars. The light was so bright that I had to shut my eyes. I kept my eyes shut, but I could feel myself still moving. A low, deep voice told me to open my eyes.

"Where am I?" I asked.

"Tommy, you have been brought to the star that watches over your family. You have been the next chosen one. Each star in the sky shines down upon a different family. With your magic ring, you will have awesome powers. These powers are to be used only to make good things happen. If you abuse these powers, the star that watches over your family will fall into a black hole, and your family will be doomed. Forever."

I had to pinch myself to make sure I wasn't dreaming. I could feel myself floating in the air. I could hear soft music playing, sounded like harps. I turned to look down, but all I could see was white light.

"Tommy, do you understand your responsibility now?" the low voice asked.

"Uh, yes. Yes I do. I must only use my powers for good things. But, I must know, what are these special powers that I have?"

"Tommy, you will learn your powers in time. Remember, only use your powers for good things."

And, just like you go down, down, down, a roller coaster at top speed, I descended down, down, down back to my papou's balcony. My stomach however, was going up, up, up. I landed back on the balcony just in time for my stomach to settle back into place. The tingling sensation finally stopped, but my mind started racing with all sorts of ideas. *I have to talk to Papou. He must know about all of this. He had the ring for years. And what kind of special powers do I have anyway? And, what did that voice mean, I learn in time? One wrong move and my family could be doomed forever. What a responsibility! I'm not so sure I like being ten anymore!*

I went inside, took off the ring, and went to bed. I slept with my eyes wide open that night.

The next morning, everyone was carrying on like normal. I just had to talk to Papou about this ring business. He must have some answers for me. "Kalimera, Papou," I said.

"Good morning, Tommy," Papou replied.

"What are we going to do today?" I asked.

"We are all going to go into town and do a little shopping," Papou replied.

"Oh," I said. "Papou, could I talk to you for a moment? Please. In private."

Papou looked a little concerned, and said, "Sure Tommy. Let's go out onto the balcony."

We walked out onto the balcony, and I took a deep breath. I wasn't sure if I was supposed to tell anyone what happened the night before, but if I could tell anyone, it would have to be Papou. "Last night, after everyone went in to sleep, I was out here for a while looking at the stars."

"Oh, isn't it great. You really do take after me Tommy." Papou said.

"Well, something really strange happened," I said. I took a few steps to close the sliding doors so that my parents couldn't overhear what I was telling Papou.

Papou looked at me and said, "What was it?"

"Something magical happened," I said, hoping he would know what I was talking about.

"Yes, Tommy, go on."

"As I was gazing at the stars, this supernatural force came upon me and sucked me up into the stars. This low, deep voice told me all this stuff about my ring having magical powers. And, if I didn't use my powers for good things, my whole family would be doomed."

Papou looked at me and told me to sit down. We sat, and I wondered what he was going to say next.

"Tommy, what happened last night is not for you to tell anyone else...ever. Only the chosen ones in our family history will have the awesome power that I once had, and now that has been passed on to you."

"So, what are you saying Papou? That you have had

these magical powers all these years and never said anything to anyone?"

"That is correct, Tommy. And, since I knew you were coming to visit Greece this summer, I thought it was a perfect time to give you the ring. I knew you would have some questions about all the magical stuff. You have to take this very seriously. As long as you remember to use your powers for good things, you will be just fine."

"Wow, Papou. This is really amazing. Now that I know what happened last night is for real, I know that I can keep my powers a secret. Is there anything else that I need to know?"

"Yes Tommy, there is. Remember to always follow your heart. You will know when to call upon your magic."

"That's it? Just follow my heart? But, Papou, what do I do? Do I have to hold the ring a special way? Do I have to wear it at certain times? How will I know?"

All Papou could say was "Just follow your heart, and everything will work."

Everyone was ready to leave, so we had to get off the balcony and on to shopping. Everything that Papou told me, kept lingering in my mind. The idea of just following my heart was a bit confusing, but I trust what Papou said. I realized that I was chosen. I was a very special boy. I was only ten years old, but I was very special. I will do just as Papou had said. I will follow my heart to do many good things for others. Papou, the ring, the magic. My tenth birthday was one that I'll never forget. I'm just wondering how all this magic will work. What would you do if you had been given Papou's magic ring? How would you use the magic?

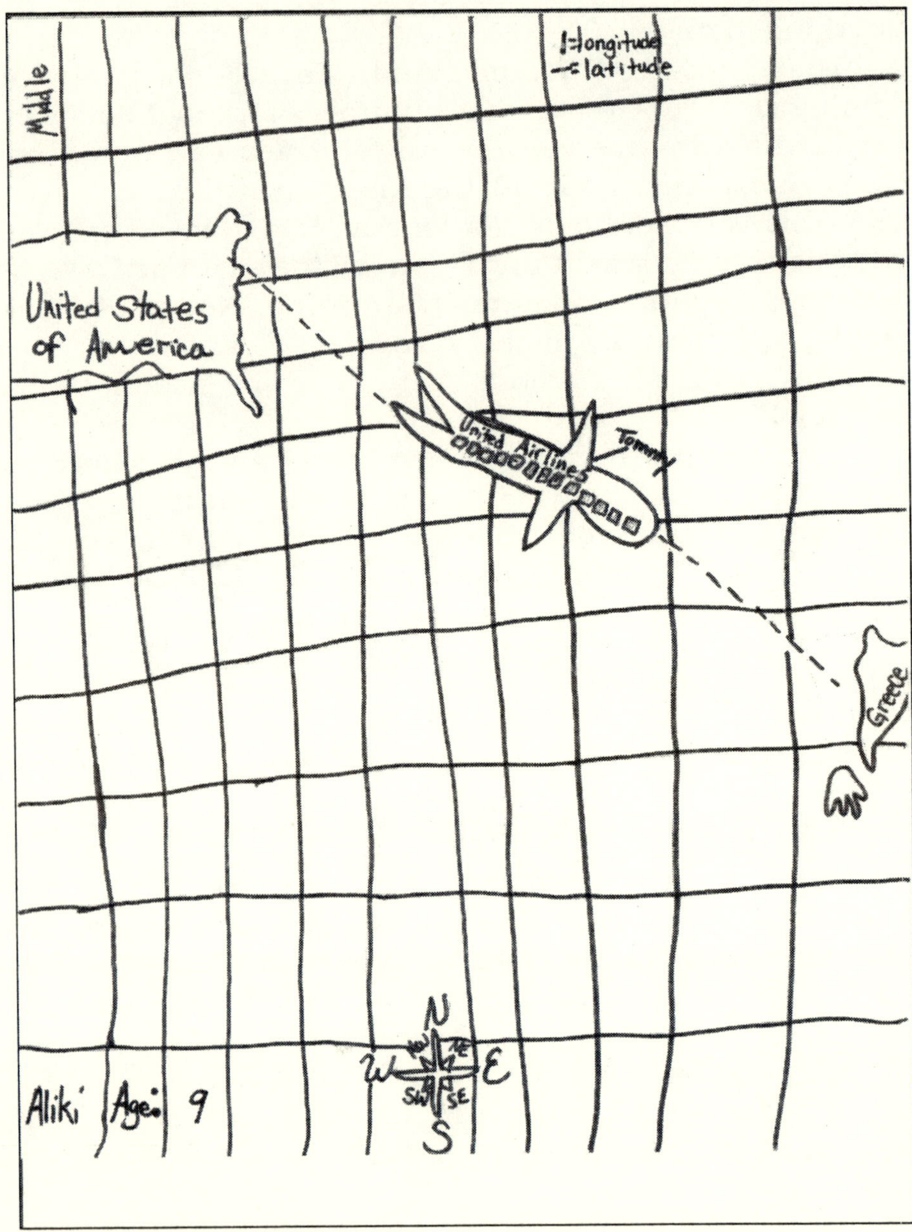
Middle
|=longitude
—=latitude
United States of America
United Airlines
Tommy
Greece
N
NW
NE
W
E
SW
SE
S
Aliki Age: 9

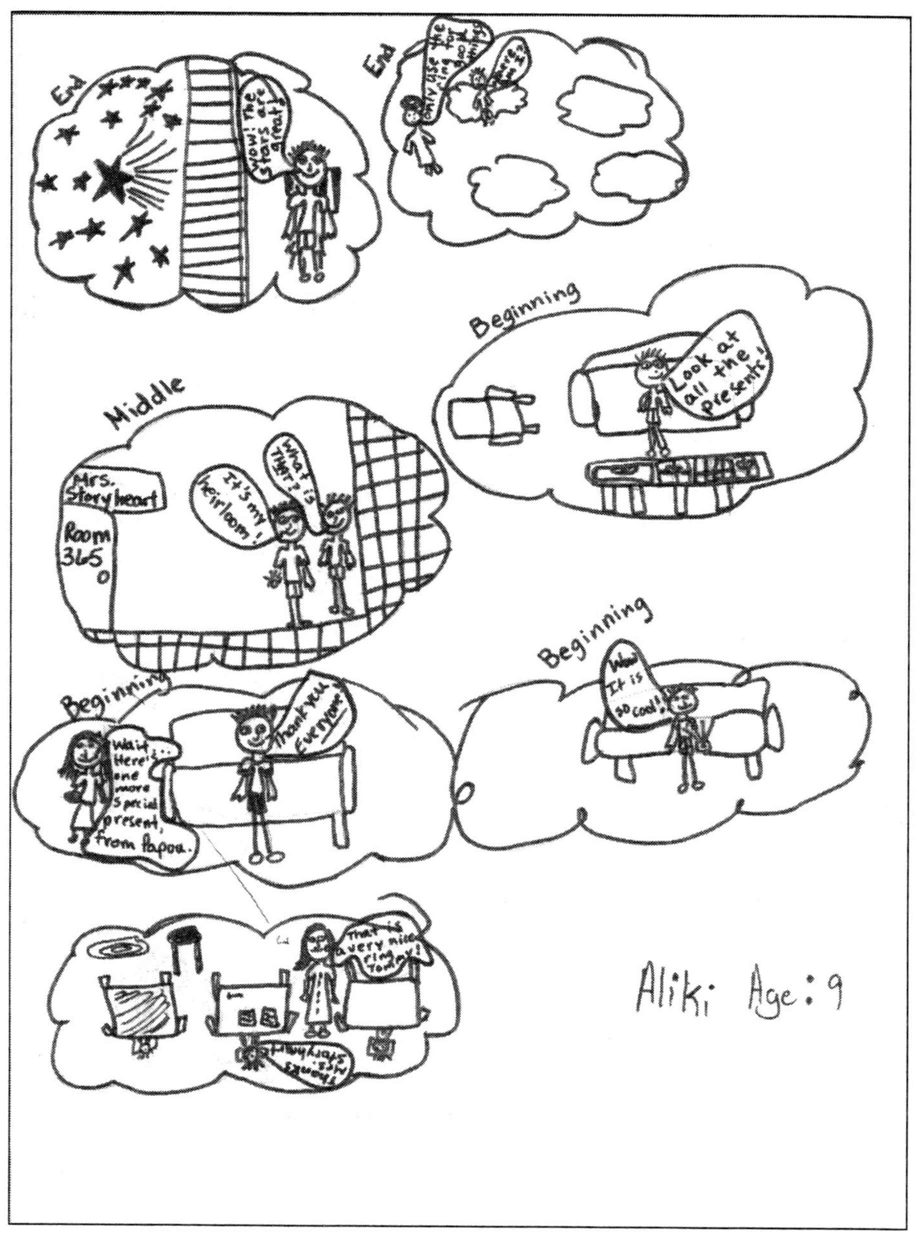
End
Wow! The stars are great!
End
Beginning
Look at all the presents!
Middle
Mrs. Storyheart
Room 365
It's my heirloom!
What is that?
Beginning
Wow It is so cool!
Beginning
Wait Here's one more Special present, from Papou.
Thank you Everyone
That is a very nice ring Tommy!
Thanks Mrs. Storyheart
Aliki Age: 9

Aliki Age: 9

One Step at a Time

By Megan J. Stoll

Another performance, another nightmare, a wreck beyond repair. She thought tonight would be different. Better. Less frightening. But, it was the same as all her other ballet recitals, for the past five years. It was plain and simple, if you are afraid of heights, performing on a stage can freak you out.

Ever since Kaily was three, she had a passion for ballet. The delicate intricacy, the grace and floating feeling, the simple joy of dancing, all made up the undeniable love Kaily had for the art of ballet.

The only thing that could overcome her love of ballet, was her fear of heights. During dance classes, she was the best of the best. But on stage, she would clumsily trip and fall. Every time she'd step out onto the stage, flashbacks of her first recital flooded her. It was as if she were there. The sounds, the lights, the visions...

It was her first recital, and they were to dance to a song from the Nutcracker. Miss Pickalee walked on stage to introduce them, "Here is the ballet for tots class performing a small version of the Nutcracker." Kaily led the class out to the front of the stage. The opening music began as they went into a plié relevé. Kaily was going into a one-footed spin, when her ankle bent and her knee went out and sent her soaring into the crowd. She took a nasty bruise on her head and a sprained wrist, but nothing serious. Still, she was in pain and couldn't stand heights thereafter.

Kaily tried hard not to be afraid, but it never worked. There was nothing she wanted more than to dance beautifully on stage. Now more than ever, she wished her fear would subside, even if it were only for one night.

"Girls, I have some exciting news," said the ballet teacher, Miss Lydia. "The company has asked us to perform the Nutcracker Ballet for the Governor and his new bride, who is former ballet dancer, Grace Addison!"

The class gasped as they sat there in awe. It would be so amazing to have Grace Addison in the audience. Instantly, they wanted to know more.

"Next class, we will learn tryout dances. And class after that, I will host tryouts," Miss Lydia said.

"Do you think I'll get the lead?" Kaily asked her best friend Alexandria.

"Absolutely!" Alexandria replied. "Do you think I'll get a good part?"

"Sure!" Kaily replied.

Kaily knew she would disgrace her class on stage if she got the lead, but she wanted it so much. Determined to demolish her fear, she started formulating a way to perform.

The next day, Kaily called Alexandria to come over before dance class. "I really need to talk to you," Kaily said.

"Sure, I'll be over soon," comforted Alexandria.

Kaily ran to get the doorbell, "Hey Alex!"

"Hi Kaily! So what did you want to talk me about?" Alexandria said as she put down her ballet bag on a chair.

"Well, you know how I really want the lead and all..."

"Yeah!"

"Um, when you said you thought I'd make it, well, I think you forgot, I don't do well on stage...the heights and all."

"I did too remember, Kaily!" Alexandria said in defense.

"Why didn't you tell me I shouldn't try out then?"

"Because I know you are the best dancer in our class and probably in the company. You can do any dance step, any routine, anything you want to do, but no one can ever see that. But, Grace Addison, she is our idol! You have to do it to show her how well you can dance. I'll help you!"

"Really? How?" Kaily asked skeptically.

"It's easy, we'll just work your way up to heights," Alexandria said in a matter of fact voice.

"What do you mean?" Kaily asked.

"Well, you can climb stairs, right? And that goes up one step at a time. So I figure, if we use higher stuff that is open too, you shouldn't be so afraid," Alexandria said with confidence.

"Well, I dunno...I guess it wouldn't hurt to try," Kaily said sheepishly.

"Great! We can start after class today!"

"Class! That's right, we gotta go!" Kaily said as she ran up the stairs to her pink room, threw on a sweater, snatched up her bag, and jetted down the stairs faster than a rocket ship heading into space.

"That was fast," Alexandria said, securing her bag over her shoulder.

"Yeah, we have like twelve minutes 'til class starts, and I don't want to be late for this class!" Kaily said.

The door slammed shut behind them with a loud thud. Two pairs of black stretch pants walked briskly on the hard sidewalk. Two canvas bags with ballet slipper appliqués slammed against Kaily and Alexandria's sides. The wind nipped their ears, but the girls pressed on, trying hard to turn the fifteen-minute walk into ten minutes.

Alexandria thrust open the doors of the large brick structure. Both Alexandria and Kaily dashed up the two flights of stairs, quickly shed their sweaters, secured their ballet slippers and ungracefully stammered into Studio 1. Miss Lydia stared at them for a few seconds. Her soft eyebrows rigid and cold, and then she smiled and said,

"Next time don't sacrifice grace for timeliness. You are early."

Miss Lydia did, however, compliment the girls at the end of class for their grace of the intricate routines she had choreographed for tryouts.

The days went quickly and before long, Kaily and Alexandria were giggling after they had tried out.

"I can see it now," Kaily said, "our shoes will glide across the floor as we are dancing in the leads."

"Yes, yes, and Miss Lydia will say our names so proudly! Ah!"

"Oh, I can't wait until next class when we find out who made what!" Kaily said.

"Yeah, me too!" Alexandria replied.

Nobody was surprised when Kaily was chosen for the lead. The only obstacle was that Kaily was declared ineligible to perform, unless she could perform on stage. *Just great!* Kaily thought. *Now how am I supposed to get this fear out of me?* Kaily frowned and her head dropped down.

"Hey," Alexandria said to her depressed friend, "Don't worry, we'll work on it, like I said!"

"Okay, but we only have eight weeks!"

"No problem, my friend. You will be dancing on stage in no time!" Alexandria encouraged Kaily.

Kaily and Alexandria worked hard. When one thing didn't work, they went to the next. Kaily's success was slow, but it was coming. Their motto became, *Keep Going for the Gold*, and that's what they did. With Alexandria's total and complete dedication to the cause, Kaily was becoming almost free from her fear of heights. Time was passing quickly.

"Kaily, just one more week!" Alexandria said.

"I know, I'm so close, but we haven't tried the stage yet," Kaily gloomily said.

"That is why today before class, we are going over to the theatre!"

"Really?"

"Yep! Grab your bag and let's get walking!"

At the theatre, their teacher, Miss Lydia was waiting. She had a kind smile on her face that reminded Kaily and Alexandria of a bouquet of flowers.

"Alex," Kaily hissed, "you didn't tell me Miss Lydia would be here!"

"I forgot to tell you, sorry. But you'll have an audience, and so she is it for now."

"Ugh!" Kaily said in disgust, "Fine!"

She laced up her slippers, took off her winter jacket, and stretched quickly. She planted her hands firmly on the rim of the stage, pushed up and put her knee onto the stage and stood up. *This is it,* Kaily thought, *I'm going for the gold. Let's do this!*

Alexandria crossed her fingers and tried to sit down, but the pressure was too much and she decided upon standing. Miss Lydia folded her hands on her lap and smiled at Kaily.

Kaily started the music, got in position, and waited for her cue. Her arms were raised above her head, she spun, she leapt, and she glided gracefully across the wooden stage. She was so wrapped up in her routine, that she saw no stage, no lights, no Miss Lydia, and no Alexandria. It was a dark theatre and she was the light. The music came to an end, and she curtsied. Kaily was back!

"Fabulous Kaily! Excellent! I've never seen you dance like that!" Miss Lydia said in amazement.

"Wow!" was all that Alexandria could say.

"You are all ready Kaily. I'm so happy for you!" said Miss Lydia after realizing that Kaily really did dance that awesomely.

The night of the recital came quickly. Kaily had the same feeling, her stomach felt as if she had eaten flies for breakfast. She froze just before she was called on stage.

"This is it, here, the gold, Grace Addison," Kaily said over and over to herself. Alexandria came up behind her and said, "Don't worry, you are the best, just do it!"

Kaily felt light, like a fairy with wings. It was her cue and she flew out. Once again she was in her own world. Every jaw in the audience dropped, Grace Addison's dropped the furthest, as they watched a graceful angel perform intricate moves so fluidly.

At the end of the performance, Grace Addison went up to Kaily and said, "I have never seen anyone better than you! Trust me, I've seen them all."

"Th....th....thank you!" Kaily was trying to find the words.

"Oh, you are just amazing! How would you like to come with me to Paris and perform with my company?"

"But, you are retired," Kaily was a bit confused.

"I can come out of retirement, can't I?" Grace said with a smile.

"Yes, but, WOW! Thank you so much Grace! Of course I'll go!"

In the audience, you could hear the crowd shouting, "Kaily! Kaily! Paris! Paris!"

Kaily turned to Alexandria and gave her a smothering hug. "Alex, I don't know how I will ever repay you! If it weren't for you, I wouldn't be up on this stage tonight!"

"Oh Kaily, don't be so humble, YOU were the one who did the dancing!" Alexandria said with excitement.

"Wow Alex, you are the best friend anyone could ever have!"

Jump
Spin
Erin Age 7

Age
Gracie 7

Green Hair

By M. A. Kokos Lambrou

The crowd was going wild! Go Henry...Go Henry...Go Henry! I could hear them scream each time my head reached above water. This was it; I had to push myself even harder now. With each stroke, I was more determined to win. I flipped and pushed off the wall for my final lap. I could still hear the crowd cheering for me. Henry...Henry...Henry...

"Henry! Get up! You are going to be late for school!" exclaimed my mom as she walked past my room. I woke up and found myself kicking my legs so hard, that I fell off my bed. *Gee, I guess that was all just a dream. If I was able to keep dreaming, I wonder if I would've won the race?* In an instant, I jumped up off the floor and went to take a shower. I didn't have much time. I got ready as fast as I could. I didn't even have time to look in the mirror. I grabbed my backpack and ran out the door. As I was on my way to school, I suddenly remembered that I had a science test that morning. I wasn't prepared for it, but it was too late now.

"Hey Henry, what's up?" asked my best friend Jonathan.

"Not much. I just remembered that we have a science test this morning. Did you study for it?" I asked.

"Looks like you practiced science on your head this morning!" Jonathan said with a laugh.

"What?" I was confused.

"C'mon Henry. Didn't you look in the mirror this morning?"

"Noooo, I overslept. I was lucky I had time to take a shower," I replied and ran to the bathroom to look at my head. What could be so bad? I took one look in the mirror, and I couldn't believe what I saw! My hair was green! Green! *How in the world did this happen?* I had to pinch myself to make sure that I wasn't having another dream. To my dismay, I wasn't dreaming. My hair really was green. I couldn't stop staring at myself. It wasn't army green. It wasn't lime green. It wasn't neon green. It was just the perfect color green. The kind of green that you see on a perfectly manicured lawn. The kind of green that you see on the leaves of palm trees. The kind of green that you see on a four-leaf clover. *After all, I am Irish. I guess I'm entitled to having the perfect shade of green, but not in my hair!* I ran out of the bathroom and into class. I didn't need to bring any attention to myself by being late.

Jonathan, however, had already gotten into the classroom before I did. He blabbed out to everyone that I had green hair. "Hey Henry, did you visit the beauty parlor yesterday?" exclaimed Jessie.

"Oh my, Henry! What in the world happened to you?" asked Scott.

Everyone in my classroom was staring at me. "I think you are a little too late for Halloween," said another classmate.

"Hey Henry, did you look in the mirror this morning?" asked another sarcastically.

"Okay, everyone. Please take your seats. It is time to get started this morning," demanded Mrs. Oakley.

"Mrs. Oakley, did you see Henry's hair?" asked Jonathan.

"Yes I did. Perhaps you should all be thinking more about the science test you are about to take, and less about Henry," replied Mrs. Oakley.

I gave Jonathan a nasty glare, and took out my pencil for the test. What a terrible morning I was having. First I woke up late for school. Then I remembered I forgot to study for the science test. And by some strange chance, my hair turned green. *I was in such a hurry this morning, maybe I used something other than shampoo in the shower,* I thought. I didn't have much time to worry about my hair, because Mrs. Oakley was passing out the science tests, and I did have to worry about that.

When I got the test, I put my name at the top of the paper. I took a deep breath and rubbed my head. I didn't know where to begin, because all of it seemed so hard. I turned the test over, took another deep breath and told myself that I would have to just do the best I could. I placed both hands on top of my head and rubbed my hands into my hair for a few seconds before I turned over the test. After I looked through the test this time, it didn't seem so bad. In fact, I seemed to have all the answers. By some miracle of a chance, all of my science knowledge came back to me. I could say that the test was actually a breeze. I was the first one done. Mrs. Oakley asked, "Are you sure you looked over your work? You finished awfully fast."

"Yes, Mrs. Oakley. I'm sure that I am done," I replied.

I went back to my seat and took out a book to read. That is what we did in Mrs. Oakley's class after we finished with a test. It was a good way for everyone to remain quiet until all the tests were handed in. Just then, Jonathan got up to sharpen his pencil and he dropped me a note. It said [*Thought you didn't study. What is the answer to number 12?*] I couldn't believe that my best friend was asking me to cheat. I put the paper in my pocket. I asked Mrs. Oakley if I could go use the restroom. At least that way if I was out of the room, Jonathan couldn't bug me for the answers. I was uncomfortable cheating. And when I saw my hair again, I was uncomfortable with that, too!

Soon enough, time was up for the test. Next we had to go to gym class. Gym lasted for forty-five minutes. I was hoping that that would be enough time for Mrs. Oakley to get those science tests graded. I was anxious to know how I did.

We started every gym class by running a few laps around the gym. Jonathan ran along side me, "Hey Henry, what's your problem?"

"What do you mean, what's my problem? What's yours?" I replied.

"Some friend you are. I asked for help on the test, and you ignored me," said Jonathan.

"I wouldn't call that asking for help. I would call that cheating. I'm not a cheater, and you shouldn't be either. Didn't anyone ever teach you that doing your own work is always better than cheating?" I was annoyed with him.

"I think that green hair of yours has gotten into your brain. You can't think straight this morning," Jonathan was equally annoyed and he ran ahead of me.

P.E. class wasn't as fun as usual that morning. No one seemed to want to pass to me during the floor hockey game. It seemed as if everyone was treating me a little differently because my hair was green, even my best friend.

When we went back into the classroom, Mrs. Oakley announced that she graded our tests while we were in gym. I was anxious to see the results. Mrs. Oakley always passed back tests faced down. She felt that your grade should be for your eyes only. She knows how nosey students can sometimes be. When I got my test, I carefully turned it over. My eyes bulged out of my head so far, that I thought they bounced down to the floor and back up again. I could hardly believe it. In big red marker it said, *100% - Superior Work!* I kept looking at my test, just to make sure I wasn't seeing things. For not studying, I really did a great job! I was a bit confused though, because I remember looking at the test and thinking that is was hard. I know I didn't cheat either. So how did I get so lucky?

After school that day, Jonathan wanted to know how I did on the test. I hardly wanted to admit that I had a perfect paper, after telling him that I didn't study for it. "C'mon Henry, how did you do?" he asked.

"How did *you* do?" I replied.

Jonathan showed me his test, "I got a 76%. If I had the right answer to number twelve, I would've gotten a better grade."

"Well, I did pretty well," I said.

"How well is that?" Jonathan wanted to know.

"Why do you have to be so nosey?" I asked.

"What's the big secret Henry? We always compare our test scores," replied Jonathan.

"By some miracle, I got a perfect score," I said.

Jonathan's chin dropped to the floor and his mouth was wide open in disbelief, "You've got to be kiddin' me!" he exclaimed.

I showed him my test. "I'm not kidding. Here's the proof."

"I don't know how you did it! Hey, maybe that green hair of yours is really good luck or somethin'!" stated Jonathan.

"What?" I asked.

"Yeah, you know, just like four-leaf clovers bring good luck. Like that," Jonathan smiled.

"Yeah, that's it Jonathan. My green hair is good luck," I said sarcastically as I rolled my eyes.

"No, really. I mean it. How else could you explain your perfect test? Listen, I have a soccer game after school today. Let me rub your head for good luck. If I play well, and we win, then we can thank your green head! How's that?" Jonathan sounded happy.

"Go ahead, rub my head. I don't think that will make a difference in your game," I said.

Jonathan rubbed my head with his hands, and he rubbed his head against mine, "Thanks Henry! I'll let you know what happens!" exclaimed Jonathan as he grabbed his backpack and ran off.

While I was walking home from school that day, I thought about what Jonathan said. Maybe my green hair did bring me good luck. After all, I am Irish. The leprechaun is considered good luck, and he is the color green.

When I arrived home, I found out that a free CD had come in the mail for me. The letter that came with it said that I was a lucky winner. *Gee, that's strange. I've never won anything before,* I thought. I went into my room to put down my backpack and try out the new CD that I had won.

"Henry," my mother called out.

"Yeah ma," I replied.

"Please come in the kitchen a moment," she said.

"Be right there." I shut off my CD player and went into the kitchen.

"I just wanted to ask you how your science...," Mom took one look at my head and exclaimed, "What in the world did you do to your hair?"

"Uh, I'm not so sure Mom. You see, it was like this after I took a shower this morning," I explained.

"Well, what did you use to shampoo it with?"

"What I always use, I guess," I replied.

"Henry, your hair is really, and I mean really green. I don't understand."

"Mom, I was shocked, too. But I have reason to think it isn't so bad. Wait here a second," I ran to my room to get my science test and the CD that I somehow won. "Look Mom, I got a perfect score on my science test. I'm honest when I tell you that I didn't cheat one bit, and I didn't study one bit, either. And look, this CD came in the mail for me today. The letter says that I won it. I've never won anything before!" I explained.

Mom took a look at the science test, "Wow, this looks great. But how...?"

I just looked at my mom and shook my head. Then I pointed to my head. She didn't seem to know what to think. Just then the phone rang. Mom answered, "Hello?"

She motioned me to come near the phone, "It's for you," she said.

I took the phone, "Hello?" I asked.

The voice on the other end was a bit cheery, "Congratulations Henry! Your name has just been selected as the winner of a brand new bicycle!"

I was absolutely stunned, "Well...what....how...? Where did you get my name from?" I asked.

The happy voice answered, "We collected the names from all the Boy Scout troops in your area and held a drawing for a new bicycle."

"Well, yes I am a boy scout. Thank you. Thank you very much. I'll let you talk to my mom, so we can find out where to pick up the new bicycle," I handed the phone to my mother.

That is the third good thing that happened to me that day. I really am beginning to think that my green hair has brought me some good luck. Maybe if all the kids at school find out about the good luck, they will be nice to me again.

Soon enough, it was time to eat dinner. Just as we were about to sit down to eat, the doorbell rang. *Uh, oh,* I thought, *if that is someone coming to tell me that I won something else, I think I'll really go nuts!* I looked through the peek hole (Mom always told us to do that), before I opened the door. It was Jonathan. *Oh boy, I wonder what happened at his soccer game?* I whipped open the door. Jonathan gave me a high-five and exclaimed, "Henry, you won't believe what happened to me at the game today! We were tied up 2-2. I kept thinking about your green hair, and I was hoping for that good luck to settle in. Sure enough, I was the one that scored the winning goal! It was awesome! Thanks Henry, you are the best! And, I'm sorry for making fun of you today!"

"Wow, that is great!" I couldn't believe what I was hearing.

"Well, my parents are waiting for me. I just wanted to share the good news with you. See you at school tomorrow," Jonathan said as he waved good-bye.

"Later," I said and closed the door. Not only was my green hair bringing good luck to me, but also to other people who rubbed off on it.

When I sat down to eat dinner, I explained to my parents what happened to me that day. They too, were in awe. My dad had one very important idea to share, "Sometimes being different is good. Now come a little closer, I want to rub that green hair of yours," he said with a smile.

The next day of school was interesting. Kids that I had never seen before were coming up to me and rubbing my head. If this continued, I was going to lose all of my hair soon. I wondered how everyone heard about me so quickly. Just then, Jonathan came walking down the hall, with a big grin on his face. *Of course*, I thought to myself, *big mouth Jonathan, who else?*

"Hey Jonathan, what's up?" I asked.

"Good morning, Henry!" he said with a smile on his face as he rubbed my head with his knuckles.

"Hey, that hurt!" I exclaimed.

"Get used to it Henry. Everyone wants to have good luck!"

I was glad that everyone in school was now being nice to me. It is strange how things work out. At first the others were staying away from me because of my green hair. And now, one day later, they can't stay away. All in all, people are silly. I'm still the same person I was without the green hair. What will everyone do if I ever decide to dye my hair blonde? I wasn't ready to find out just yet.

Age 7

Ah!
Gracie Age 7

Froze Zone

By Megan J. Stoll

"And the Bears lead it 21 to 6 in the fourth quarter," the television blared.

"Oh yeah! That's right, kill 'em! Bye, bye Patriots!" Ty said.

"Bears winning?" asked Tabitha.

"You betcha! The Patriots are awful this season!" Thomas chided.

"That's it guys. No more TV. You're going to get sucked in if you watch anymore," their mother, Mrs. Taylor Mitchell, said as she passed by the family room.

Ty turned off the TV as he groaned.

"Yeah, yeah, moan all you want. Now all three of you come into the kitchen. I need you to agree on a birthday list and details," Mrs. Mitchell said.

All three kids sat down at the island, their feet dangling.

"Here," their mom said as she slid three tablets of paper and three pens across the smooth, granite countertop, "Now, first things first. You each can invite seven kids. Anymore and I would die."

The kids quickly wrote down the names of their friends.

"Done!" Tabitha yelled. Her dog Tinnie Tia scampered to Tabitha's chair, begging to be picked up. Tabitha reached down to pick up her black and white Havanese puppy.

When everyone finished their lists, Mrs. Mitchell gathered them up and reviewed them. "Okay. Your lists look fine. Now, where might twenty-one fourth graders like to go for a birthday party?"

"In the TV!" Ty said in a sarcastic voice.

"I have no doubts that you would enjoy that," Mrs. Mitchell said.

"How about to Paris?" Tabitha suggested.

"Ruff, ruff," Tinnie Tia added.

"Well, I don't think the boys would like that, would you?" asked Mrs.Mitchell.

"We could go play laser tag, and then swim at the pool," Thomas suggested.

"Yeah!" Ty and Tabitha said together.

Mrs. Mitchell set the date for the next Friday after school. Meanwhile, the triplets talked nonstop about the upcoming party.

The next morning at 7:00, Ty plopped down in front of the TV to watch his favorite show. "Yeah! I love this one!"

Tabitha walked in wiping her eyes. She blinked, "Oh my Ty, wait, no, Thomas, what are you doing?"

"Gosh, are you that tired? I'm not Thomas, I'm Ty!"

"Right. Sorry." Tabitha sat down in a large overstuffed brown leather chair. Then Thomas walked in, still in his super hero pajamas.

"Morning," Yawn. "Tabitha, Ty, ah, how could I forget Tinnie Tia and Truth?" Thomas said as Tabitha's dog and the family dog, a black lab, came to greet him. Thomas pulled back the curtains to reveal four large cherry french doors. For the first time that morning, they saw it. Huge mounds of soft, sweet, pure drops of heaven.

"Ahhh, looks like a snow day!" Ty roared.

"Yes. Yes, it does. Unfortunately, you guys won't be permitted outside because it is going to be twenty below zero," Mrs. Mitchell commented as she went to make pancakes.

"Ohhh well, at least there are some good shows on this morning," Ty said.

"Yeah, until the baby shows come on," Tabitha added.

"Hey, the sports channel is on all morning," Thomas said.

Mrs. Mitchell poured the thick, creamy pancake batter onto the burning hot griddle. The pancake sizzled, fizz, zzz. Ty walked into the kitchen. His elbow rested on the side of the counter. His eyes gazed longingly as those pancakes took form.

"Smells good Mom," Ty complimented.

"Thank you honey. Just wait until you taste them with whipped prune sauce!"

"What? Eeeew! Whipped what?!"

"I'm just pulling your leg honey. Kids, could you put some cocoa on the stove? You need a little warmth. Tabitha! Thomas! Need your help!"

****

"Mom makes the best breakfast, doesn't she?" Tabitha commented as they all walked into the family room. Each of them sat down and cuddled up with a cup of steaming cocoa and a warm blanket.

"Cool! Back to backs! Gosh, his stupidity is so funny!" Thomas said.

"Yeah," Ty and Tabitha replied.

"Wouldn't it be cool to be inside a TV show? A cartoon, like this one, too!" Ty said with his eyes glued to the TV.

"Oh, Ty. Honestly honey, do you have anything better to do?" Mrs. Mitchell said, carrying a laundry basket to the basement.

"I can't hear. Could you turn it up?" Thomas asked Ty.

Ty reached for the remote. His thumb rested lightly on top of the "up" button, as if it were instinct. He pressed the lower edge of the rubber button, and the top of the "down" button. All of a sudden there was a bright light, sparks, and a glowing tunnel.

"Ahh! Ty!" Tabitha screamed.

"What the heck?" Ty yelled.

"Uh, oh," Thomas said dully.

"Ouch!" they all exclaimed.

"What was that?" Thomas asked.

"Where are we?" Tabitha added.

"I think we...we...we're inside the TV!" Ty sputtered.

"Oh great! Don't you just hate it when Mom's right? How does she always know? It's like magic," Tabitha groaned.

They looked around. Everything was a cartoon. The sky was a dull green, and the ground was gray blue. They had gotten themselves inside their favorite cartoon.

"What did you do?" Tabitha asked with a cold rigid voice.

"Hey, I'm sure we can figure a way to get out of here," Thomas said.

"Guys, I'm sorry. But is anyone feeling cold?" Ty said while holding his elbows and shivering.

"Oh great! Did you forget where we are? We're in Froze Zone! It is always cold and always snowing!" Tabitha yelled in fright.

"Oh no! Here comes Finko!" they all said.

A huge marshmallow came running towards them. His red-white teeth were sharpened to a point, and his huge bullet-like eyes were fixated on the Mitchell triplets.

Seconds later Ty asked, "Whoa! Where are we?" as he blinked his eyes furiously.

"It appears like we are...we are...inside Froze Zone!" Thomas said stunned.

"Oh no!" they all exclaimed.

Ty had a large gash on the side of his right shoulder; the blood looked like a huge red gum drop with little sugar crystals on top. His head was cut badly from the left temple to that area just below the nose where there is a slight pucker. On the ground was Tabitha's leg, all twisted like a piece of malleable wire.

"Oh my gosh!" shrieked Tabitha in horror, "Look at your head!"

"My head? What about your leg?" Ty said motioning toward a pale white thing with a cinnamon candy cane stripe running down the middle.

"That needs to be taken care of right away!" Thomas said in an urgent, terrified manner.

"Oh, what happened to us?" Tabitha asked, "We look like Garry Deli did after Finko..."

"We've been Finkepied!" they said in horrified unison.

They all thought. How could they get out? What would they eat? And the question on Thomas' mind alone, *What book is like this?*

Tabitha kept remembering the episode where Finko attacked Papa Snow. If only she could try to escape as he had, but she couldn't. There was only one Papa Snow, and there are three Mitchell children. Her idea would only work for her. Hmmm? *Should I go and create a plan to only save myself?* Tabitha wondered. But deep down in her heart, she heard a tiny voice saying there is another way. How? How could all three of them be saved from Finko? His evil was surrounding them.

I know! thought Thomas, *If I would just follow the steps of Igor the Mighty...Oh, dang it! Igor hadn't had to save his two siblings though. Hmmmm.....*

An eerie silence surrounded them all. It was like a thick blanket coating them from head to foot. They had difficulty breathing.

"Ta cucu, bith mmm a," Ty coughed.

"Mmm," Tabitha struggled with invisible monster, "What?"

"Do you feel something?"

"Yeah."

"I think Finko, I think he...aw how do I ...we've been gued!" Thomas said sounding out every syllable with disgust.

"We've what?" Ty and Tabitha screamed.

"Sorry," Thomas said, "but, yessss! We are going to die. Okay? I love you guys, see you in..."

"Thomas, get a grip!" Tabitha demanded.

"She's right! You will die if you don't cut it out!" Ty said sternly.

The clear sticky gu had Ty, Tabitha, and Thomas

pinned up against a nearby tree. No one could escape this horrible stuff. Even if you were not starved to death, the gu would eat away at your body. Any cut from Finko attracted thick gu blankets. Thomas had completely given up. Ty was discouraged, but Tabitha had the courage to keep hope alive. What so quickly killed her brothers' determination, gave her energy.

"Ja Ja Wieshctein!" Tabitha proclaimed.

"Tabitha, I want a quiet departure please," groaned Ty.

"No! Wait! You know the episode with Ja Ja Wieshctein and the Weigshin Brothers, and how they tried to escape the gu? Yeah, well they had a Giant Hydro Jercometer 900 Special Deluxe Unlimited Gold Silver Platinum Edition!" Tabitha said in one huge breath.

"Where will we find one of those?" Thomas asked absent mindedly as he starred into the dull green sky.

None of them knew where to look for one, not even Thomas! All of a sudden, they heard a low rumble. Tabitha looked up at the sky. It couldn't be another attack from Finko, could it be? They all ducked their chins and said their good-byes, then closed their eyes and awaited destiny.

One eye open...the other... "Are we...alive?" Tabitha asked.

Ty and Thomas opened their eyes. "Yeah, I guess we are!" Ty said stunned. Thomas was speechless. There it was in front of him. Ty and Tabitha looked over at him.

"Whoa!" Tabitha said in amazement, "A Giant Hydro Jercometer 900 Special Deluxe Unlimited Gold Silver Platinum Edition!"

"No way!" Ty screamed, jumping up and down.

This machine was the latest in cartoon technology. The show had just been aired the day before. It's chrome trim made the gold sheet metal look super techy, and all the knobs and tubes made anyone who looked at it want their mommy, but not the Mitchells!

"This is our ticket out of here," Thomas said reaching forward only to be reminded of his guey prison.

The way the Giant Hydro Jercometer 900 Special Deluxe Unlimited Gold Silver Platinum Edition works is simple. All you have to do is wish it to go into Mellowed Mode and feed it some courage, and voila! Home free!

"Guys, 'member how this thing works?" Thomas asked.

"Uh...oh yeah! Wishing!" Tabitha joyously shouted.

"What do we wish?" Thomas said, looking puzzled.

"Hmmm," Ty was deep in thought.

Tabitha pressed her lips together and strained her eyes trying to see something with her eyes closed. It was coming to her, come on, little closer...there! "Mellowed Mode! Wish it to Mellowed Mode," Tabitha said.

"And feed it courage!" Ty added.

"Ready? On three," Thomas said.

"One...two...three!"

Ty tried really hard. His eyebrows came closer, leaving a tuck of skin in between. Thomas closed his eyes and smiled. They might have a chance after all. Trying hard not to overdo it, Tabitha wished herself blue. If she had gone without restraint she may have blown up!

Next, they heard a faint teakettle whistling. It was growing louder, stronger, a menacing sound. How horrible! It reminded Tabitha of her mom's tea with green leaves and orange ginseng. Home. That is where Tabitha wanted to be right now. Instead, she was stuck in guey, messy, marshmallow glob. What a way to spend a snow day!

The machine gave out a "rump," "kabokshaboom," and "thud!" Five huge tubes came towards them. They looked like huge snakes staring at you directly in the eye. The teakettle sound started up again. A sound similar to a vacuum was having a contest with the teakettle sound. Louder, nail biting, ear shattering, wretched sound! Ty could not stand one more second of it! At the top of his lungs he shouted, "Stop! Shut up! Please! No more noise. I can't take it!"

Somewhere during all the yelling, it subsided. And

suddenly, all that was heard was Ty's yells. The gu was gone. All gone. Free at last!

"We can move!" Tabitha gleefully said.

"Yes, and the noise stopped!" exclaimed Ty.

"Odd. Very peculiar," that was Thomas.

Still, one problem was yet unsolved. How were they to get home?

Over yonder, there was a tree coated in white fluffy snow. The branches were sheltering hands grabbing at the sky. Thomas had the idea to try to make camp over there. It was a good enough spot. The tree kept the wind from chilling them, and there were some scattered branches and nuts on the ground.

"Not bad bro!" Ty exclaimed.

"Thanks."

All three scurried about creating a shelter low to the ground to trap heat. The branches they covered with more branches until a super thick shelter was built. On top, Thomas had said to pack snow. Lots of layers of branches and snow helped to create the warm fortress. It was even camouflaged, so Finko would have a hard time finding them. Tabitha looked at the dark crevice in the tree, "I wonder what's in here. Maybe an animal home?"

She carefully stuck her hand in the crevice. As she felt around, she could make out a jagged object. It was almost like rubber, but it was hard in some places.

"Ty, put your hand in here, I found something," Tabitha said. At that moment, a feather would have easily shattered her.

"Hmm," Ty said, feeling around, "I don't believe it! I would know this thing anywhere!"

"What?" Thomas and Tabitha asked excitedly.

"A remote control!"

"I don't believe it!" Thomas said.

"Ya better!" said Ty.

Ty snatched the remote out of the crevice and immediately started pressing random buttons. In fury and disgust, he thrust it down. He thought hard trying to remember which buttons he had keyed in before. Nothing worked.

"Weren't you trying to turn up the volume when this happened at home?" Tabitha asked.

"Yeah, you were!" Thomas shouted.

"Okay, I'll try it."

As soon as he said this, his fingers jumped to that in between spot. Bright lights flashed as the Mitchell triplets were transported back to their family room!

"There you guys are! I have been worried sick! Where were you?" Mrs. Mitchell said in rage.

Ty looked at Tabitha, and Tabitha looked at Thomas. They shrugged and said, "You were right Mom. By watching TV for so long, we did get sucked into it!"

"Right guys. You have a great imagination!"

Cassie Stamas.
Age: 9

Glob
Age 7
Erin

Giant Jercometer
900 Special Deluxe
Unlimited Gold Silver
Platinum Edition
Gracie Age 7
Gracie Age 7

Erin
Age 7

"Froze Zone"
Age 5

A Second Language

By M.A. Kokos Lambrou

Every Saturday morning, it was the same routine. I had to go to Greek school. Most other children my age were at home watching cartoons. But me? I had to get up at 8:00 a.m. to be at Greek School by 9:00 a.m. Each week I tried to delay as much as I could. I would sleep as late as I could. And, it never failed, each Saturday morning; I would have a tummy ache. I would stay in the bathroom as long as I could. Each Saturday, I was always late for Greek school.

"Samantha, let's go now!" Mother called.

"I'm coming," I replied as I gathered my books.

"Samantha, I just don't understand why you dislike going to Greek school each week. It is a wonderful opportunity for you to learn a second language," Mom said this almost every week.

"I'm just no good at it Mom. All the other kids in class are so much better at it than me," I said.

"Oh, stop worrying about those other kids. Just do your best," Mom said as she pinched my cheek and smiled. I did not smile back.

Before long, we arrived at the church where I took the lessons. I think my teacher was aware of my pattern of lateness each week.

"Kalimera, Samantha," my teacher said.

I usually responded in English, "Good morning."

I took my seat and looked at the clock. I had 2 and a half hours to go.

We were practicing conjugating verbs. It was all so confusing. The verb started with the same sounds, but the endings were changed to show if we were talking about you, her, him, they, we or us. It is so different from learning English. All the other students in class already knew how to speak the language pretty well, because their parents were from Greece. I, on the other hand, was starting from scratch. My parents were both Greek, but born in America. They knew how to speak English very well, and that is how they spoke to us at home. They still knew how to speak Greek very well, too. The other students in class were there mainly to learn how to read and write the language. After conjugating the verbs, we were practicing various sounds of the Greek alphabet.

I had trouble making the "r" sound in Greek. In order to make the sound, you had to curl up your tongue to the roof of your mouth and push it through. The result, *rolling* the "r" sound. My teacher called upon me to say the word "Kalimera," which means good morning. *Oh, great. A word that has an "r" sound in it.* I tried as hard as I could, "Ka – li – me- th –aaa." When I tried to roll the "r" sound, my tongue landed between my teeth, and I sprayed all over my desk. The other students in the classroom were giggling. My face turned so red, and felt so hot, I thought my head was going to explode like a volcano! "Almost!" my teacher responded with a smile. "Why don't you give it another try Samantha?"

So I did, "Ka – li – me- thhh – aa." Once again, the "r" sound did not roll, but landed all over my desk. Once again, I felt embarrassed and left the room. I heard the other students giggling as I left. I went to the bathroom and put cold water on my face. That was the worst. I just hated being different from the other kids. Didn't they have a special class for students like me who had trouble making the "r" sound in Greek? I put more cold water on my face, and headed back into the classroom.

I looked at the clock. Two more hours to go. My teacher didn't ask me to say any words with the "r" sound in it for the rest of the morning. I thanked God for that.

As class continued, I noticed that the two boys sitting next to me were only pretending to read their Greek books. Behind their Greek books, they had comic books that they were reading. I so badly wanted to tattle on them, but they already thought I was different; I didn't want to stir up any trouble. I was trying to pay attention to what my teacher was saying, but the boys sitting next to me distracted me. It just wasn't fair. They weren't even trying to learn anything, and they already seemed to know everything. I, on the other hand, couldn't even get my sounds straight.

Once again, I managed to get through my whole class without learning much. I did give myself credit, however, for writing the Greek letters pretty well. That was something I could do, because I didn't have to say it. Not soon enough, it was time to go. I ran outside to my mother's car. "Mom, guess what," I said.

"What?" she asked.

"You know the two boys in my class, Robert and Leo?" I asked.

"Yes."

"Well, I caught them doing something bad today," I was satisfied I could tell somebody.

"Oh yeah? What's that dear?" Mother wanted to know.

"When we were reading from our Greek books, I saw that they had comic books behind their Greek books, and they were reading them the whole time! My teacher never caught them!" I exclaimed.

"Well, Samantha, don't you get into anybody else's business now. Like I tell you each week, you need to worry about doing *your* best. How did you do today?" Mother somehow turned it around back to me.

"Me? Not so good. I'm still having trouble rolling my "r" sound. I tried it twice while the whole class was listening, and I sprayed all over my desk, twice! I was so embarrassed Mom! Now do you understand why I don't like going to Greek school?" I was angry.

"Samantha, honey, I know that this has been difficult

for you. But trust me, you will be thankful that you learned another language when you grow up. Why don't you concentrate on the things you do well at in Greek school. I know that you write your letters very well, and that you can put down a few good sentences on paper," Mom was encouraging.

"I guess so Mom. I'm hungry, what are we going to eat for lunch?" I asked, trying to change the subject.

"I thought we could go try that new restaurant that opened up in town. How's that?" she asked with a smile.

"That sounds good," I replied. Mom always seemed to know what to say and do to make me feel better. As we rode to the restaurant, I thought about what she said. I thought about my ability to write Greek words and sentences. Maybe she is right. Maybe I need to start focusing on the things that I'm good at first, instead of punching myself in the stomach for what I can't do.

During lunch, I talked with my mom about many different topics, but of course, the subject of Greek school came up. Instead of my mom lecturing me about how wonderful learning a second language was, she encouraged me to try writing more Greek. She told me that I had a great imagination and that I could turn some of it into stories, in Greek. She said that she would even help me. I actually kind of liked the idea. As long as I didn't have to roll "r's" in front of anyone, I think I would be fine.

When we got home that afternoon, Mom was anxious to start helping me pen a story in Greek right away. I had to keep it simple, since my vocabulary was limited in Greek. All in all, I created a cute little story, with Mom's help. The story was about a little rabbit that moved to a new town and had to make new friends. At first, the little rabbit had trouble making friends because he was different. The little rabbit had a gift of making others laugh. Once the other rabbits discovered his gift, they quickly became friends. The moral of the story is to give everyone a chance. We all have something to offer.

I was pleased with my story. I was anxious to share it with my Greek school teacher the following week. I was just hoping that she wouldn't ask me to read it out loud to the rest of the class.

One week later, it was time to go to Greek school once again. This time, I wasn't late. This time, I walked in five minutes early. I thought my teacher was going to fall off her chair when she saw me.

"Kalimethaa," I said.

"Well, Kalimera Samantha. What a pleasant surprise to see you so early."

I smiled, "I have something to share with you. I wrote this story at home and I was wondering if I could share it with the rest of the class."

"Well, of course Samantha. That would be great!"

"Oh, one more thing. I'm a bit uncomfortable reading it out loud. Would you mind reading it for me?" I asked politely.

My teacher sighed and said, "I guess that'll be all right."

Right at 9:00 a.m. all the other students started to arrive.

"Kalimera, class. We are ready to begin. I'd like to start out this class a little differently today. I'd like to start by reading you a short story."

All the students took their seats and they were attentive.

My teacher read the story aloud to the class. I was really proud of my work. I was wondering if she was going to give me the credit for writing the story.

After she read the whole story, Leo raised his hand and asked, "What book is that story from?"

My teacher looked at me, I nodded, and she said, "The author of that story is sitting right here in our classroom." She pointed to me, and everyone started clapping. My heart was smiling inside. I was so proud. The rest of the students really liked it. That was a great way to start class that morning, because I started to feel a little more comfortable conjugating those verbs. And, I really didn't care that Leo and Robert were looking at comic books behind their Greek books.

I learned something really important about myself that day in Greek school. I learned that I should focus on the things that I can do, instead of the things that I can't do. I discovered that I can write Greek well, and others who heard it, enjoyed it. I decided that I will continue to write Greek, and that I was going to put forth more effort to those things that were hard for me. I was determined to learn my "r" sound. I was now determined, and I was now ready to learn the Greek language.

STOP FAKING! You are going!
My stomach hurts!
Aliki Age: 9

Angelica Age: 10
You're not to read the comic books! You are to read your Greek books!
Angel
So what- we like comic books
Yeah!
RM.27
Be back in 5 min. kids! I have to get some paperwo
Also- read your read-ing books while I'm gone!

Angelica Age: 10
How did you do today?

Angelica Age: 10
Aliki Age: 9

Stove
Mom I learned something very important today at Greek School
What did you learn?
That I should focus on the things I can do instead of the thing I can't!
Well I am glad you learned that.
Aliki Age: 9

Ella Finn the Elephant

By Megan J. Stoll

Her slightly chubby fingers knocked over a small picture frame that lay on her nightstand while trying desperately to press the snooze button on her alarm clock. Ella wasn't very happy that her mother had once again set her alarm clock. She pulled the yellow and pink quilt over her head and went back to a peaceful sleep, hoping her mother wouldn't come to see what was taking her so long to get ready for school.

"Ella, Eleanor! Wake up sleepy head!" a freshly-baked-batch-of-cookies voice said over the intercom system.

The young girl reluctantly got out of bed and pulled on a black shirt, faded to gray, and a pair of elastic waistband blue jeans. Ella pounded down the wooden steps moaning and groaning, making her brother Toby scream at her to walk quietly.

"I'm coming, Mommy. But why do I have to go? Can't you just home school me like Kelsia's mom?" Ella said, not expecting an answer.

"I can't skip work honey. Doctors are very important to people, and I like my job. Maybe you can like yours, too? What do you say?"

"No, no, no! You don't understand! All the kids, oh just, ugh!" she said blowing out a gust of breath.

Ella dug into her stack of buttermilk pancakes, dripping in butter and drenched in pure maple syrup. She stuffed her face with the delicious food, leaving a ring of syrup on her upper lip.

"I'm glad to see that you are enjoying your breakfast, but can't you slow down?" Ella's mom said with a hint of amusement.

Ella kept on eating. Her cheeks were full and she still tried to cram more into her little mouth. An occasional "Mmm," and "Dranks," (thanks) came out of Ella's mouth.

"Oh, honey I forgot to tell you, Dad says good-bye and sends his love. He's going to be in Turkey for a month. Some big project, I suppose," said Ella's mom.

Ella didn't slow down. She didn't even acknowledge that her dad was gone for a month.

"Ella, I see that we enjoyed Mr. Snooze Button today. What? Three, four times? Oh my," Ella's mom sighed, "What am I going to do with you?"

Ella looked up sheepishly, "I dunno."

****

"Ha! Look at her! She even looks like one," snickered a boy as Ella walked by.

"Yeah, she is so fat that she's blocking my view! Bret, Bret, where are you?" said another boy sarcastically.

Ella's head hung down as she desperately tried to hide the little lakes that had formed below her eyes. She tried to ignore them, but they surrounded her. It was like she was a basketball player coming through the gate, but instead of reporting good statistics; they reported how much she weighed and how much she resembled an elephant.

It's not like Ella is mean; in fact, she is very nice, it's just that the kids at school only cared about how good a person is at sports, how skinny they are, and how popular they are. Ella paints and draws stunning pictures, and she helps out at the dog shelter by feeding and walking the dogs. Unfortunately, no one cared about the inner beauty of her.

She didn't have any friends at school. They all made fun of her size and name. "Ella Finn the elephant!" they would chant. Some days, Ella felt like it would be better just to give up.

She did have one friend however, Kelsia. Kelsia is Ella's cousin, her best friend, her only friend, and a very good poet. They were inseparable ever since the day they were born. Their houses were right next to each other and they did everything together. Then one day, Kelsia's family had to move. Ella cried and cried. She keeps some of Kelsia's poems under her bed in her treasure box, along with a scrapbook they made. Whenever she gets sad, she reads the poems, and the world doesn't seem quite so bad. Kelsia's poems are like magic.

Ella took her seat in Miss Jibson's fourth grade classroom and put her books in her desk. The rest of the class did the same thing. Miss Jibson took out her dry erase marker and started writing on the wipe-off board.

Today's Agenda

1) **Gym Class**
2) **Social Studies**
3) **Art**
4) **Recess**
5) **Math**
6) **D.E.A.R. (Drop Everything And Read)**

Oh no! Ella thought, *not gym class! I hate gym class!* Ella was slower than everyone else, she was clumsy, and she never was picked for teams. The rest of her class used her slowness and clumsiness to taunt her even more.

"Okay class, settle down," said the gym teacher, Mrs. DeCrosse. "Now, who'll be today's captains for basketball?"

Twenty-five hands fluttered in the air, some waving wildly, while others were slightly more polite. Bret and Tucker started to jump up and down. The only hand that wasn't waving, belonged to Ella. Mrs. DeCrosse looked around the gym with her hand stroking her chin and her eyes squinted. Ella stared at the linoleum floor, concentrating on all the different shades of blue. Mrs. DeCrosse never picked Ella as a captain and for that Ella was deeply indebted to her.

"Mmm, let us see, how about, hmm, well... Oh! I know, Ella and Bret! Come on forward guys," said Mrs. DeCrosse.

Bret let out a quick hurray and did his little victory dance. The class cheered for him because he was a great captain and the best basketball player. Everyone wanted to be on his team.

Ella moaned as she slowly stood up and shuffled to where Mrs. DeCrosse was standing. *How could she do this to me?* Ella thought.

The class was silent with the exception of Tucker who shouted his disapproval of Ella, "Oh come on Mrs. DeCrosse! You know this'll be a super quick game. I mean, Bret against Ella? It's a no brainer!"

Bret picked first, "Tucker!" he shouted as they gave each other a high-five.

"Uh, Jessica," said Ella so quietly that Jessica could hardly hear her.

"Oh man! I wanna be on Bret's team though!" Jessica moaned.

The picking of teams continued with happy shouts from Bret's team and moans and groans from Ella's team. Ella's cheeks felt like a burning hot burrito every time someone would say how bad she was. To further her embarrassment, Ella couldn't even win the coin toss for which team had to wear the smelly pinnies.

Mrs. DeCrosse held the ball up in the air. It seemed like Bret's shoes were equipped with mini jet packs. Ella could hardly get her feet off the floor before gravity tugged at her. Bret's team had the ball. They scored, scored, scored, three-pointer, scored, rebounded, and scored. Ella's team had only 5 baskets, all of which were from free throws.

"This team stinks!" shouted Jeremy as he threw down the ball at half time.

"Yeah we're terrible," commented Jessica.

Ella just hung her head. It wasn't like it was her fault; she was just one bad player. Why did they keep blaming her?

Mrs. DeCrosse's whistle blew to signal the start of the third quarter. Ella's team got deeper into the hole, losing by ten, twenty, and thirty.

A stampede of basketball shoes ran towards Ella. They yelled and shouted; their hands waved madly in the air. *What are they doing? Why are they running towards me?* Ella thought frantically. It was then that she realized that she had the ball. By some chance of luck, the ball had landed in her chubby hands and now she was going to die from it. They came closer and closer until finally they were on her.

Bret knocked the ball out of her hands and Tucker shoved her to the ground. Ella's team tried to regain control of the ball, while Bret's team was jumping up, ready to rebound. Ella covered her head and prayed that no one would land on her. Her leg hurt really badly, like somebody had a voodoo doll of her and was sticking needles in them.

"Ouch," Ella silently whimpered.

She didn't feel like getting up. It was too hard to do. Giving up would be so much easier.

Ella's eyes started to open once the sound of pounding feet became fainter. She was lucky that she didn't get stepped on, because she was right under the basket. Ella stared blankly at the blue padded wall in front of her. She picked out the red and silver EXIT sign among all of the blue.

Then, an idea sprung in Ella's head. She could just run away. Ella figured she would be able to make a run for it out the door, and then she could walk the rest of the way. Where she would go, she didn't know. All Ella knew was that she didn't like school, gym, or her classmates.

If I run to Kelsia's house, then Aunt Tara will call my mom. I could live in a motel for a while. No, that wouldn't work. Hmm, I know! I can live in my tree house in the forest and then sneak food whenever I need to.

Ella had her plan all worked out. Mrs. DeCrosse was out of the gym and the game was still at the other end. Now all she needed was a quick and unnoticed exit. She slowly picked herself up and snuck over to the door. She slowly pushed open the door and held it as to assure a slow, noiseless close. She was out!

The big oak tree out on the parkway beckoned her to come nearer. She decided to rest under the tree for a few minutes. Ella began thinking.

I wonder what my mom will think. She'll be really sad, and I'll miss her, too. I don't think Toby will miss me very much and Dad already misses me because he's in Turkey. But they just don't understand. No, they don't. I can't go back to school. Today, gym class was so humiliating! Giving up is so easy. Hey, wait a second, that is what some of Kelsia's poems are about, how giving up is easy, and you should never quit.

Ella recited a few of Kelsia's poems. She wasn't so sure if she wanted to run away anymore. If she ran away then she would be quitting, but if she didn't, then she would be miserable still. This decision was a tough one!

The oak tree shaded Ella from the brutal sun as she contemplated whether or not she should run away. *I can't give up. What would Kelsia think of me then? All she ever writes about is not giving up and overcoming your obstacles. I shouldn't run away. Nope, I'll walk back into the gym. Class is probably almost over, and if I am not caught, then I'll put on a good face for the rest of the day.*

Ella quietly opened the door. The game was almost over, and her team was still losing. She crept in like a caterpillar and took a seat on the bench. Mrs. DeCrosse wasn't in the gym at the moment and Ella was very glad. Ella tried to hide her face when Mrs. DeCrosse entered the gym for fear that her absence was noticed. Luckily, it was not.

The rest of the day she heard the normal remarks, but

ignored them. She was like a shield and all of their arrows bounced right off.

****

Ella hopped out of her mom's silver Mercedes station wagon and walked as fast as she could to the kitchen phone. She dialed Kelsia's phone number and prayed that she was home.

"Yellow?" a perky voice at the other end said.

"Um, hi, its Ella, can I speak to..."

"Ella? Hey, what's up?" Kelsia cut in.

"I just wanted to talk to you, if you have time."

Ella told Kelsia about her whole day. She asked her what she should do. After all, Kelsia had to make new friends when she moved and some of them made fun of how poetic she was. Kelsia told Ella something that her mom had said, whenever they say something mean just say, 'Why do you feel the need to tell me that?'

The next day at school, Ella tried that line. She knew that her Aunt Tara always gave good advice, but she didn't really expect this to work. However, when Bret and Tucker started the whole, "Ella Finn the elephant" chant, she said it, and they were stumped. They didn't know what to say. Bret stuttered and stammered, while Tucker stood there with his jaw on the floor.

Eventually, the teasing ceased, and Ella was able to make friends. She laughed and played like a 9-year-old should. Occasionally, Bret and Tucker would try to start up the "Ella Finn the elephant" chant, but all Ella had to do to stop them was to say her magic line, "Why do you feel the need to tell me that?" and she also remembered Kelsia's poems.

There was a dream I once did have,
the wish of a fool.
A goal that I would someday reach,
and show the kids at school.

It made me happy; made me cry,
and looking back I see,
That dream was written in my soul
and was what made me, me!
So still I try to reach that star,
and complete what I've begun,
And someday soon I guess I will,
and my battle will be won.

Gracie Age 7

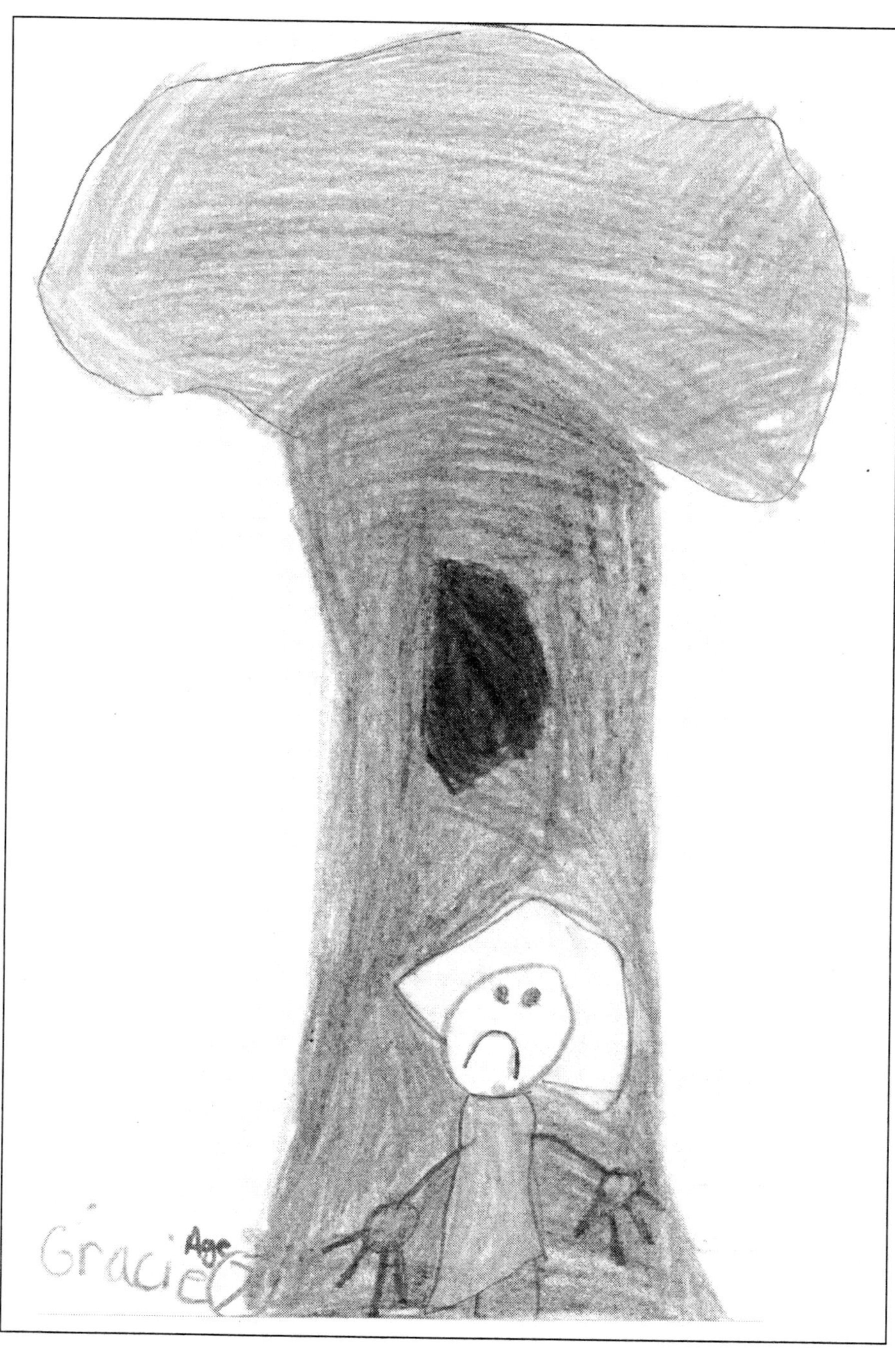
Gracie
Age

Ella Finn's

Treasure Box

Poems by Norah Scannell

As I sit here all alone,
I look around and sigh,
For everybody laughs out loud,
and now I wonder why.
I feel alone, afraid, unsure;
I don't know what to do,
So I sit here by myself, and then I find you.
You make me laugh,
and make me see how good my life can be,
To feel the joy and spread it;
to let everybody see.
To let people know me, and not to be afraid,
And to look more at the good things,
and not mistakes I've made.
I love you now, I loved you then;
I'll love you all my days.
Because you've touched my life and saved
me, in many special ways.

Your smile melts all dark around me,
Your eyes set the world aglow,
You take my hand and help me,
but I never really know.
You help me through and lead me on,
just like a friend should do,
And I'm so safe and happy, all because of you.
So thank you friend, I love you now,
and until the end is here,
I'll help you through like you helped me;
in light we'll fight the fear.

A secret blooming garden, a little apple tree,
I'm gonna find a special place,
and make it just for me.
I'll go there when I'm angry, and when I'm very sad,
You can't come in, unless I say;
not even mom and dad!
I'll write a secret password,
and make a special sign.
This place will be so perfect,
and it will be all mine.
Inside will be a grand estate,
with butlers, maids and all,
There'll be a swimming pool of ice-cream,
and a shopping mall.
Yep! That secret place of mine,
oh it will be so great!
I'll enter through a carriage,
and through a golden gate.
So now you've heard of this great place,
oh it will be so grand,
And whenever I'm unhappy,
I'll go to my special land.

There was a dream I once did have,
the wish of a fool.
A goal that I would someday reach,
and show the kids at school.
It made me happy; made me cry,
and looking back I see,
That dream was written in my soul
and was what made me, me!
So still I try to reach that star,
and complete what I've begun,
And someday soon I guess I will,
and my battle will be won.

There's a fear that's growing in my heart,
I'm alone and I am scared,
Time has pulled my feet from under me
and left me unprepared.
Now fear and pressure pull me in,
In the dark I sit and cry,
Until you reach down with a helping hand,
And pull me to the sky.
You smile and then I know
that it will turn out all right,
So I thank you, friend, for saving me,
from the wicked night.

When I see you all around me,
I feel safe, and I feel glad,
I love you all so much,
you're the best friends I've ever had.
I'm always glad to see you,
as I hope you are for me,
You never fail to make me laugh,
best friends we'll always be.
I'll help you through your sorrows,
and cry when you're in pain,
And I'll share in all your joys with you,
as we have more to gain.
Our friendships are so special,
so every single day,
I'll be standing here by all of you;
I'll never go away.

A little pink flower, standing all alone,
One tiny fragile flower,
with no place to call its own.
So small and frail and helpless,
it stands so cold at night,
But it grows and makes us happy,
and tries with all its might.
Alone it stands, but strong it is,
and lovely as can be,
This one teeny tiny flower might be
stronger now, than me.

A fire that's burning in the night,
A star that's shining clear and bright.
So brave and bold it will shine through,
But that same fire can burn in you.
You can be bold and brave and right,
And lead the way with all your might.
Courage will flame, and it does burn,
So through our lives we all can learn,
That to be right and to be true,
You need the courage found in you.

A day that sunshine won't light up,
And makes you cold and blue,
Can be turned around and changed,
So you are happy, too.
Every frown can be a smile,
And happy you can be,
If you just focus on that ray of hope,
And just trust that it will be
A day that's filled with joy and love,
And will be remembered 'till the end.
Because if you want, you can be happy,
And that's why you are my friend.

If a smile can take away a frown;
A laugh take away a tear,
And a little word of confidence can take away a fear,
Then why not do that always,
and make the whole world smile,
So every day of every year,
would be worth the while.

Someone to stand by you,
and to help you see the light,
Who's standing right there by your side,
to make sure it's all right.
They'll be there in your darkest hour,
even when you give up hope,
And even when they are unsure,
they will help you cope.
They'll laugh when you are laughing,
and weep when you are sad,
And will love you and protect you,
even when their world is bad.
And when you mess up somehow,
they'll forgive, and they'll forget,
Because they are a friend of yours,
and won't give up just yet.
And after years have gone by
and in Heaven you both meet,
They will still be there beside you,
to help you to your feet.

I look around and see them all,
standing in a line,
They smile, and laugh, and they love life,
these great friends of mine.
They greet me with a hug,
every morning, every day,
And each of them has touched my life,
in a special way.
Some of them are always happy,
and some of them can sing,
But every single one of them
keeps me beneath their wing.
They shelter and protect me, make me laugh,
and make me cry,
And I'll love them all forever,
friendship will never die.

A little tear of joy,
trickles down my face,
Because I'm just so happy,
in your warm embrace.
I'm so blessed to know you,
and to be here with you today,
I don't think that I could stand it,
if you went away.
We will be friends forever,
no matter what the cost,
And we will stand by each other;
We never will be lost.

Your smile and rays of sunshine,
pierce through the darkest night,
Then we walk off hand in hand,
towards a shining light.
Friends until the end,
I will stand by your side,
I trust you so completely,
in you I will confide,
My hopes, my dreams, my pain, and fears,
And you'll tell yours to me,
And forever after, best friends, we'll always be.

Jumping up and down,
I think I'll touch a star.
My life is so wonderful,
and I have come so far.
I've come through joy,
and come through pain,
And though it's true I've lost a lot,
I have so much more to gain.
I have friends who'll always be there,
no matter what the cost,
And without them and my family,
I'm sure that I'd be lost.
I love the past, I love right now,
I love what is to be,
I'm going to live my life and love it,
oh so happily.

A heart of gold the boy did have,
And a soul so pure and true,
That all who looked upon him loved him,
And of his goodness they all knew.
He'd been through pain and sorrow,
but still loves all his life,
And at every opportunity,
tried to put an end to strife.
The boy had friends and family,
and people he could trust,
And every aspect of his life,
It seemed so fair and just.
But this boy, he had a secret,
That he bore with pain,
Because it caused him such great sorrow,
But he knew he had to gain.
He kept on going with a smile,
'cuz in the end he knew,
That the good in life outweighed the bad,
and to that you must be true.
So remember friends, that ever life,
a bed of roses may not be,
For every rose will have a thorn,
that you cannot always see.

A note from the authors...

All of the stories in this book have a common theme: the characters had to overcome an obstacle. They were all able to do it by helping each other. Although the stories in this book are all works of fiction, we hope that you apply the lessons of helping others, and perseverance towards your own life. We thank you for supporting Bear Necessities Pediatric Cancer Foundation, Inc.

ABOUT THE AUTHORS

"If I had only one wish, I would wish for the cure of all forms of cancer," says Megan Jeanne Stoll, whose cousin, Larry Dunn, was diagnosed with pediatric brain cancer at twenty-one months of age. "It's so devastating to watch the effects of any form of cancer." Larry luckily was able to overcome the devastating disease with the help of a wonderful family, friends, excellent doctors, major medical advances, and Bear Necessities Pediatric Cancer Foundation, Inc., which provided a swing-set for him when he was no longer able to go to the park. Larry is now a healthy, happy five-year old whose valiant fight has touched many hearts and inspired thousands of people. Thank you, Larry, for showing so many people how to "Bear the Challenge."

Megan is 13 years old and resides in a suburb of Chicago, Illinois. She competes in triathlons as well as numerous runs. She loves writing, sailing, and playing the piano, and thanks her Grandpa, Larry Dunn, for his revising and editing expertise.

Norah Scannell is fourteen years old and lives in Illinois with her parents, sister, and brothers. She loves to write poetry, and gets her ideas from her own experiences as well as those of her friends and family. Norah sings in a local church choir and has done several recordings with them. Spending time with her friends and family, as well as playing the guitar, piano and harp are some of the things Norah enjoys.

M.A. Kokos Lambrou teaches elementary school, and teaches fitness classes for adults and children. Lambrou met Stoll and Scannell when they were her students in her elementary classroom in 1998. Stoll and Scannell are also students in Lambrou's kickboxing classes. The three decided to collaborate on this project for the good of the children. Lambrou says, "It's been a real joy collaborating with past students on such a worthy cause." Lambrou is currently working on a sports and fitness book for children, and she is the author of WWW.WINGS, a chapter book for third grade and up, also available from Llumina Press. Her website has valuable information for both kids and adults, www.makokoslambrou.com.

For more information about Bear Necessities Pediatric Cancer Foundation, visit their website at: www.bearnecessities.org

A special thank you to all of the child artists.

Larry Dunn Age: 5

Aliki Mitsiopoulos Age: 9

Angelica Mitsiopoulos Age: 10

Erin Ploen Age: 7

Gracie Ploen Age: 7

Cassandra Stamas Age: 9

YES, I want to help make a difference.

Please accept my donation of $________ to benefit children battling pediatric cancer,

Donation From: ____

Address: ____

City: ______________________________ State ____________

Zip __________

Please make check payable to: **Bear Necessities PCFI**
For credit card payment: (Circle One) **VISA** **MasterCard**
Card Number: ____

Expiration Date: ____________

Note: If your company participates in a Matching Gift Program please include the form.